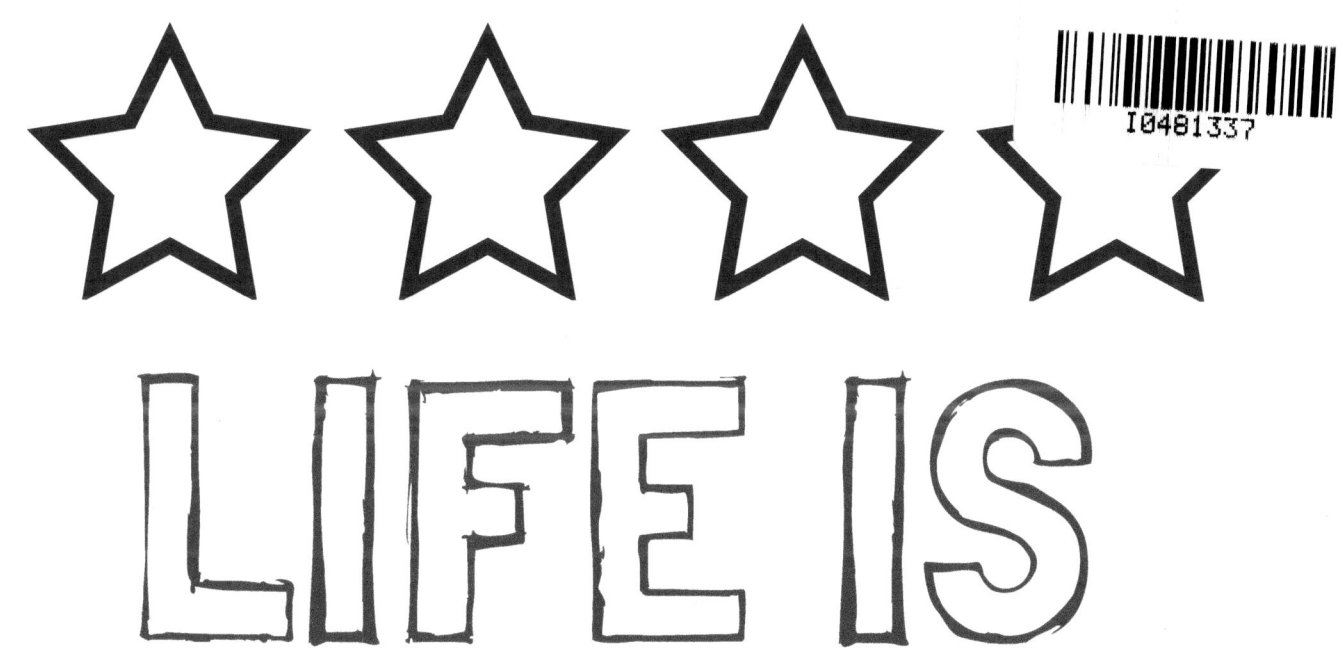

LIFE IS

what you

MAKE IT

☆ ☆ ☆ ☆

PEACE

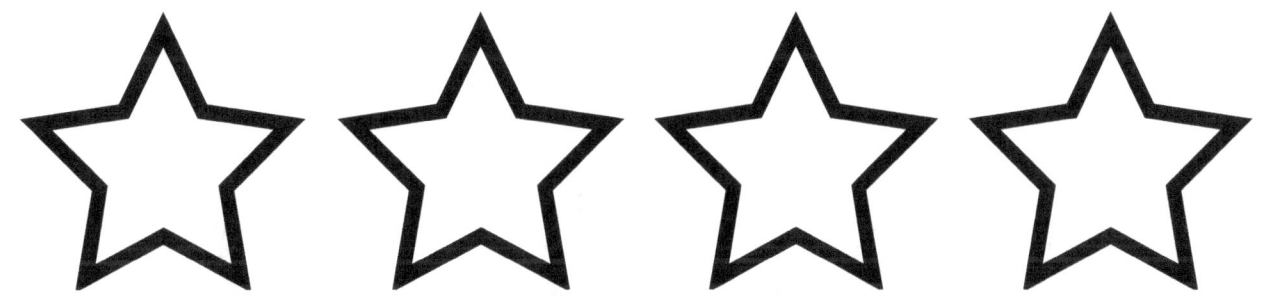

HAPPINESS

is

OUT THERE

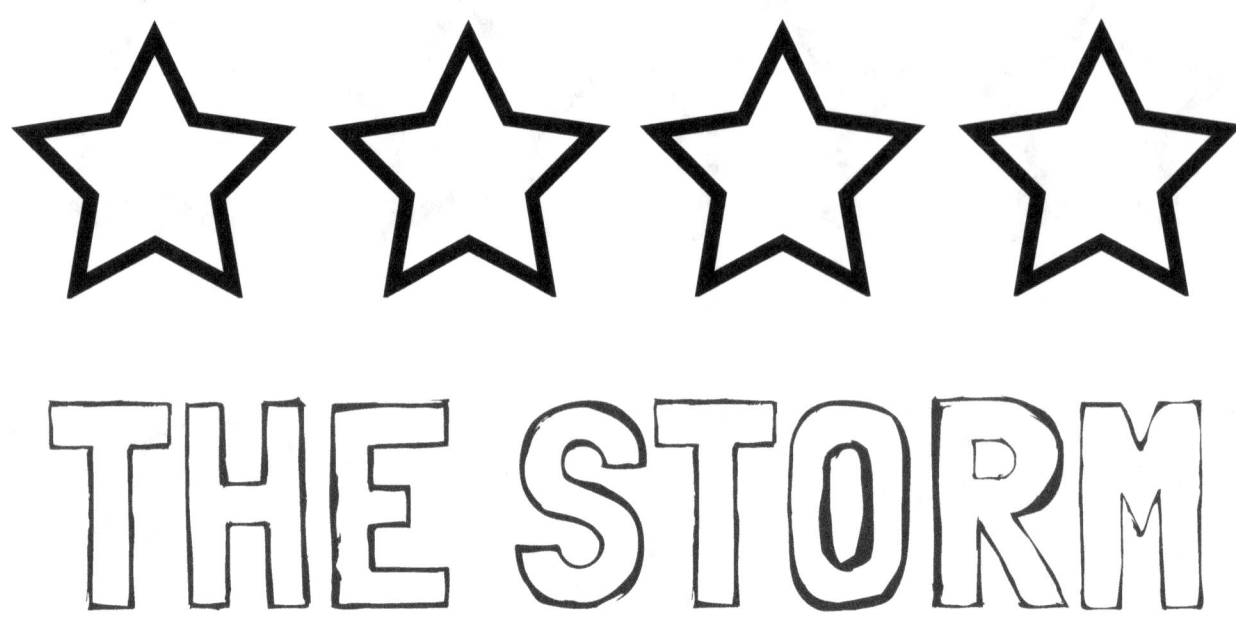

THE STORM

comes

before

THE CALM

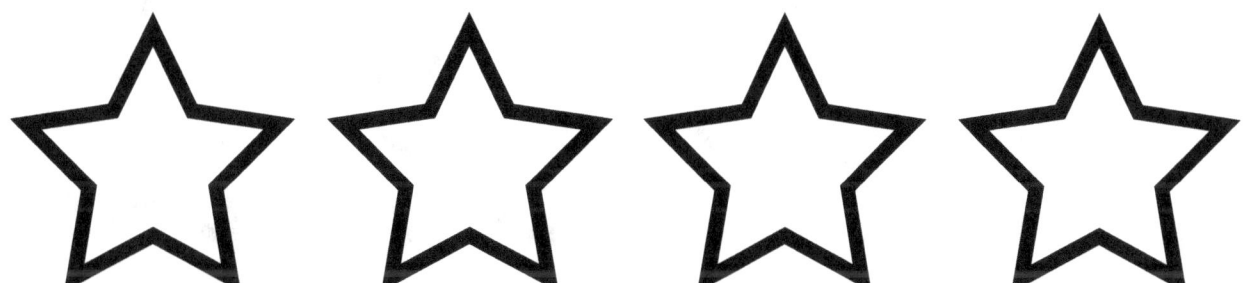

TODAY

is a

GOOD DAY

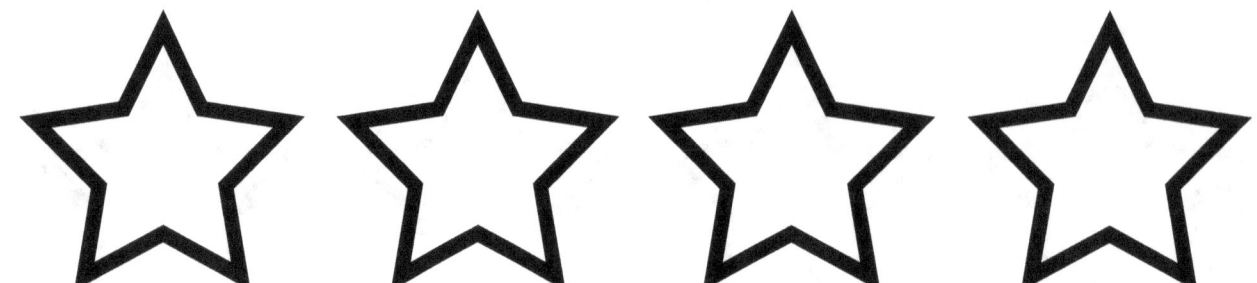

NEVER

STOP

BELIEVING

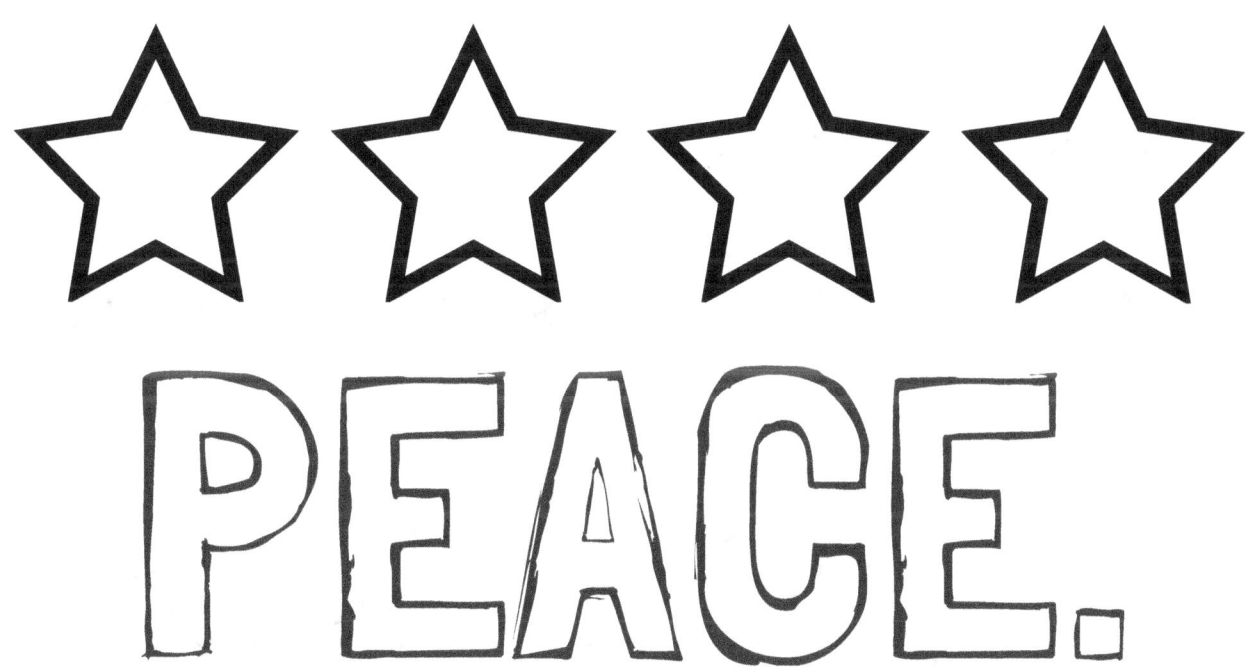

PEACE.

LOVE.

HOPE.

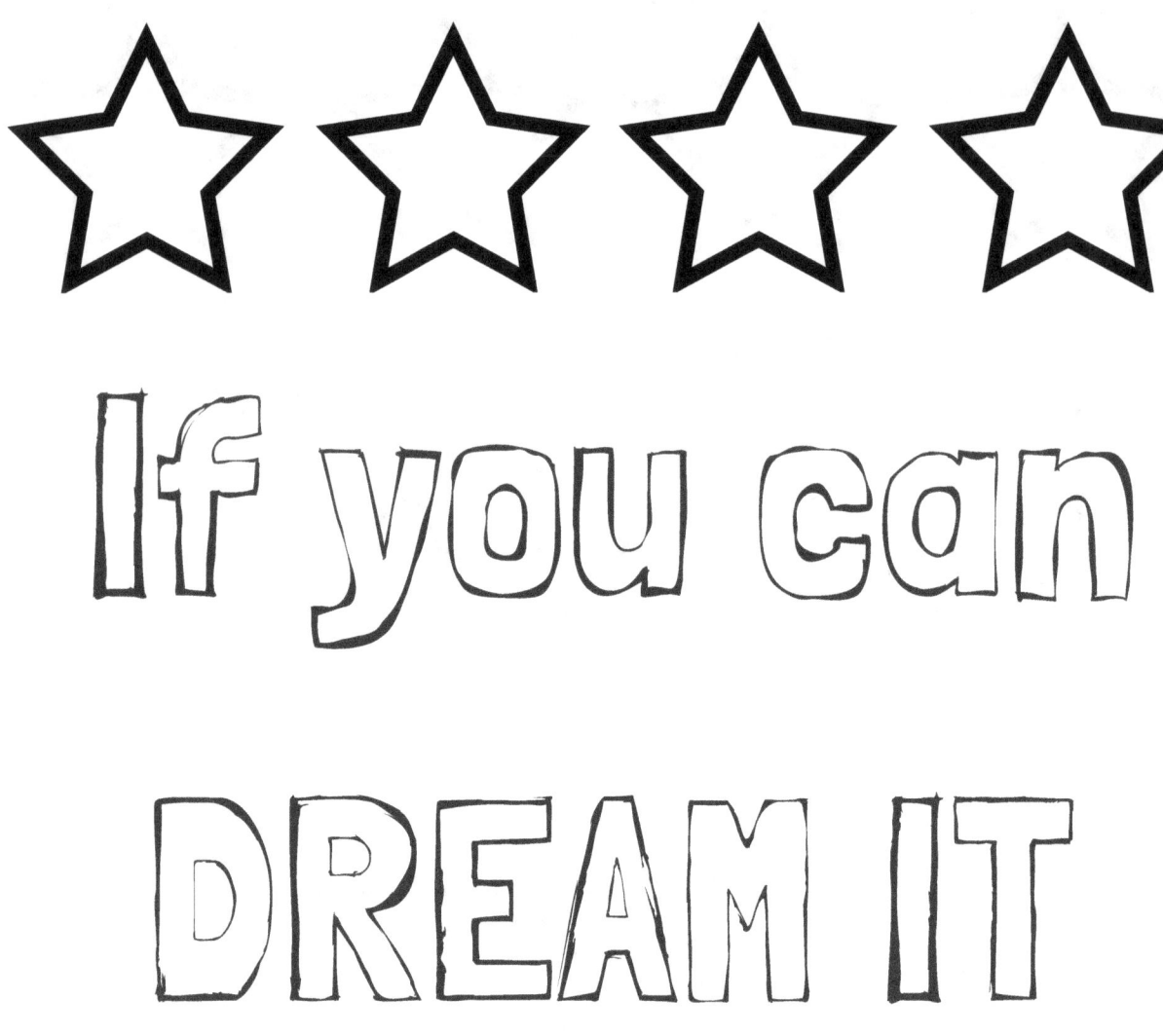

If you can
DREAM IT
you can
DO IT

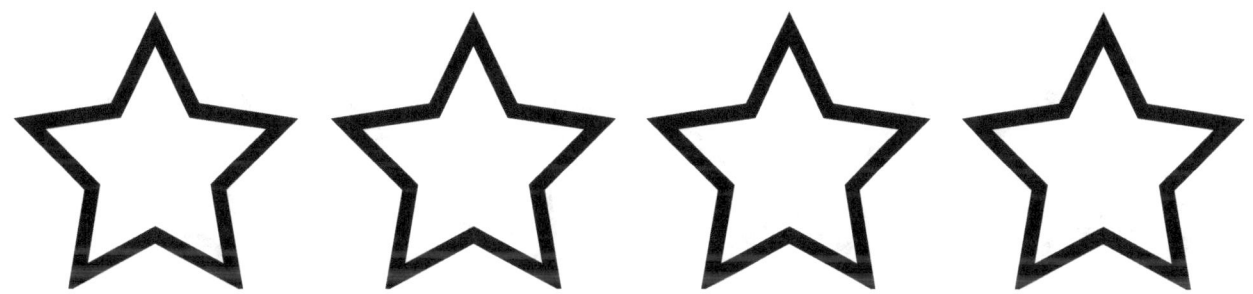

WHATEVER YOU ARE BE A GOOD ONE

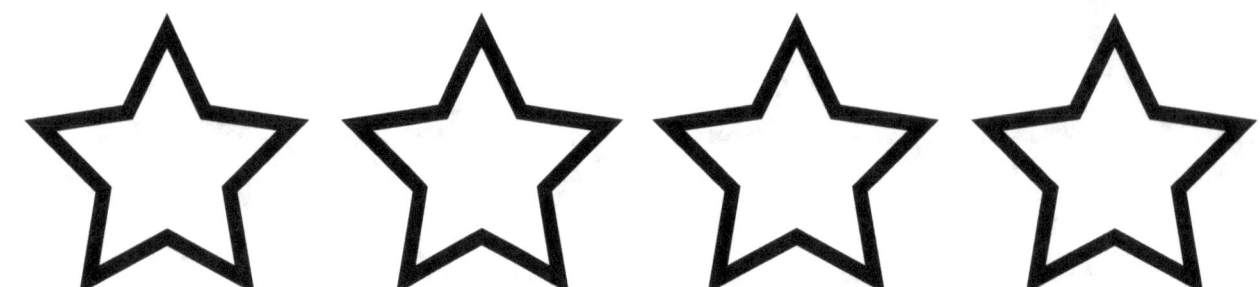

NEVER

NEVER

ever give up

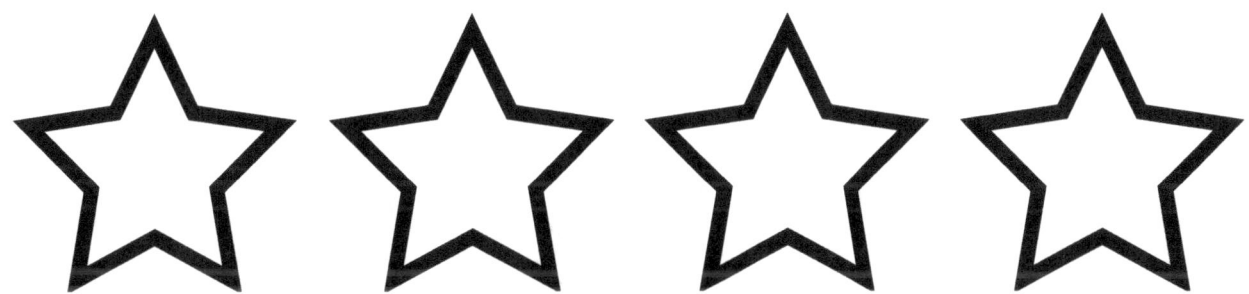

EVERYTHING

you can

IMAGINE

is real

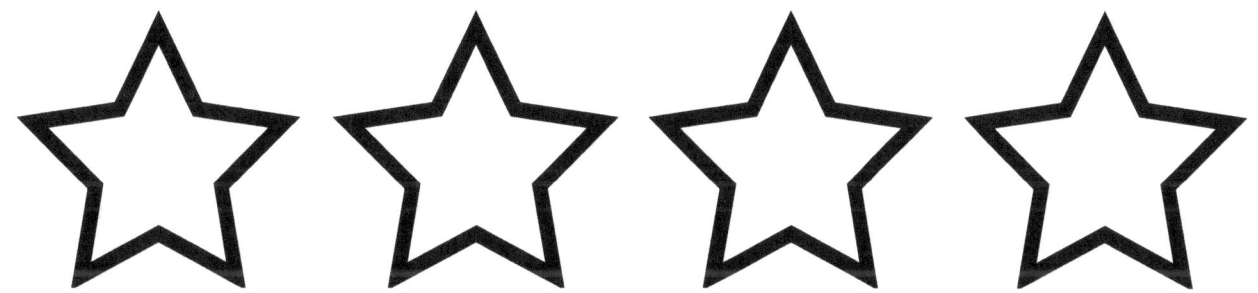

BE YOU

BE BEAUTIFUL

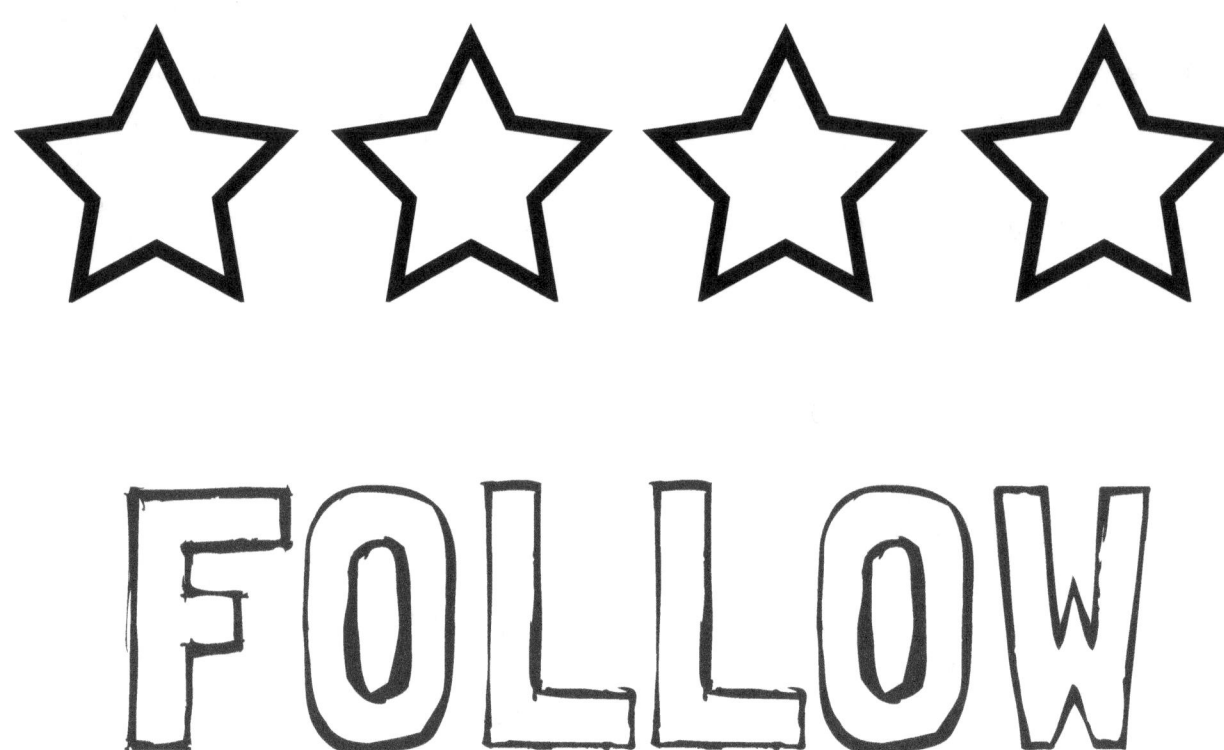

FOLLOW

your

BLISS

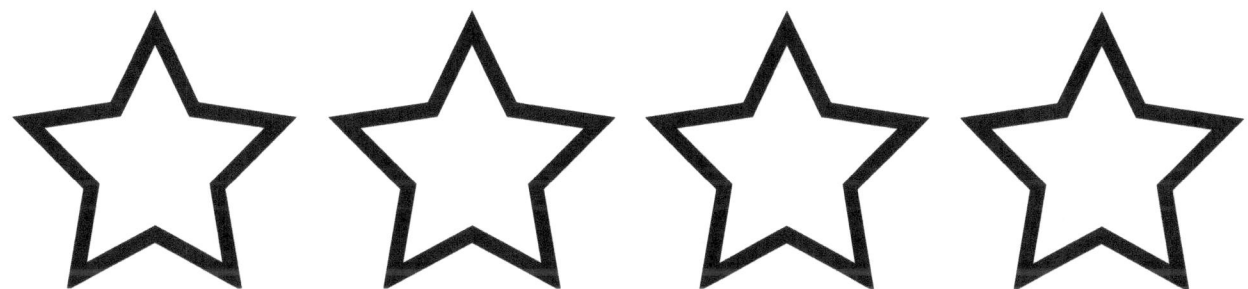

TURN
wounds
into
WISDOM

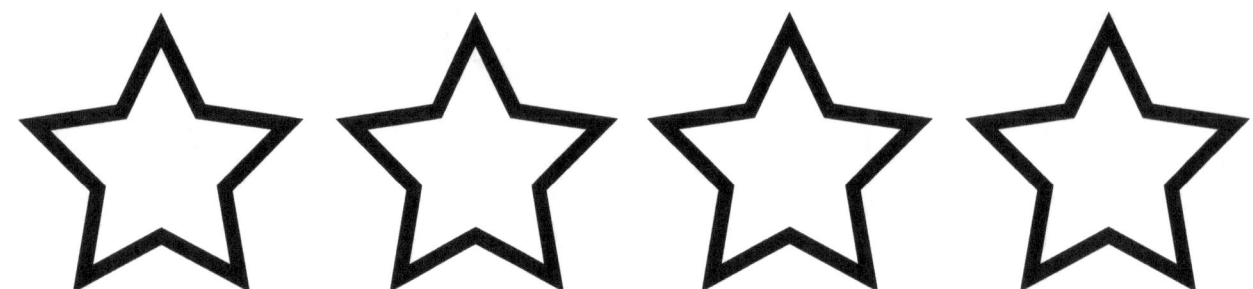

HOPE IS
A WAKING
DREAM

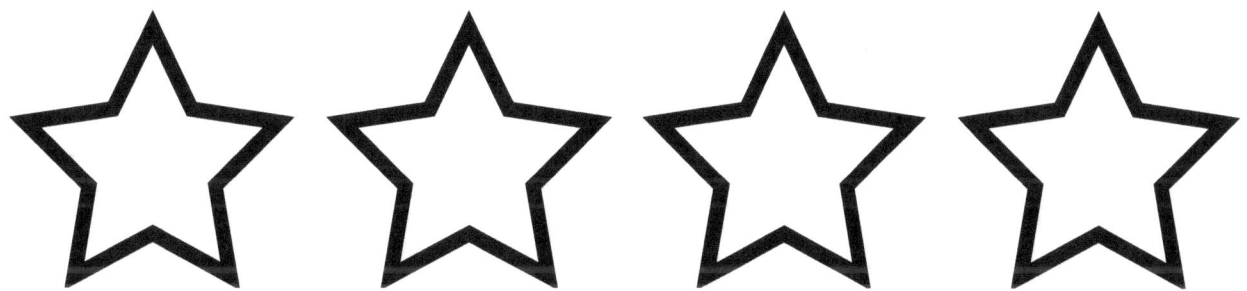

DON'T REGRET

the past

ONLY LEARN

from it

☆☆☆☆

LIVE WHAT YOU LOVE

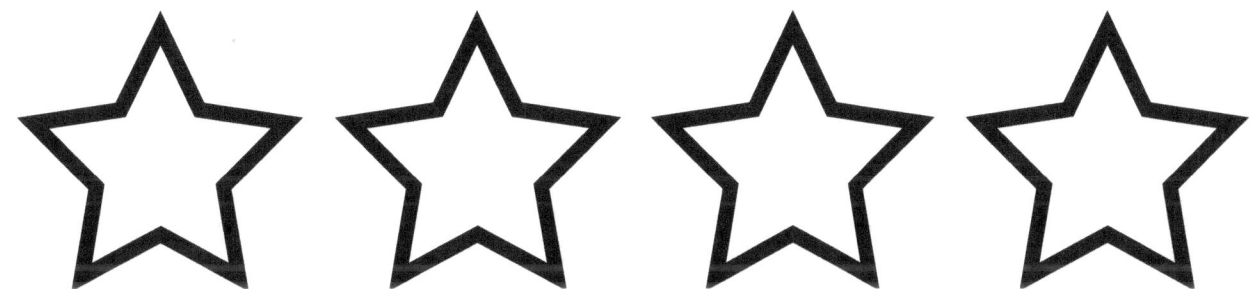

A JUG

fills

DROP BY DROP

THE OBSTACLE

is the

PATH

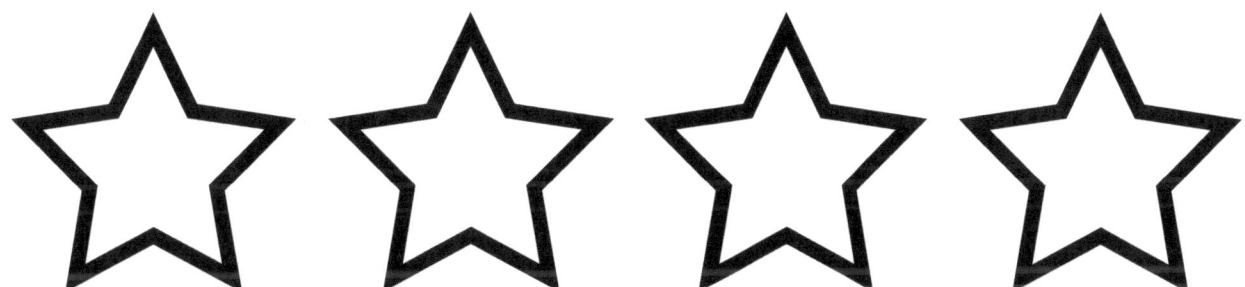

HOPE

is the

HEARTBEAT

of the soul

ALL YOU

NEED IS

LOVE

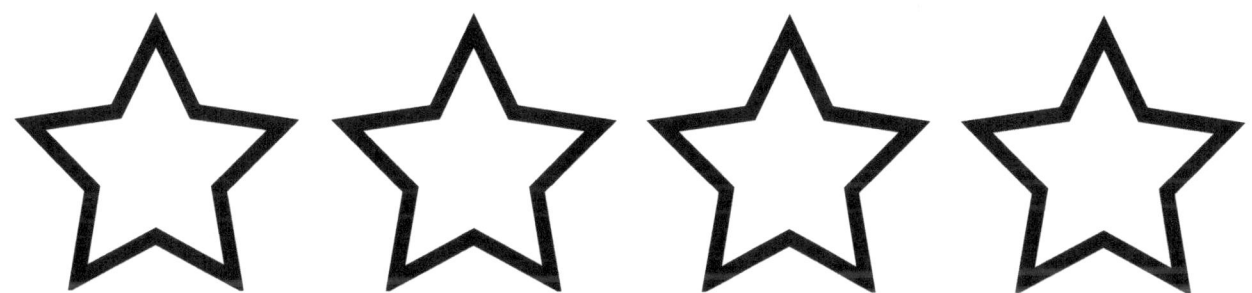

WE BECOME

WHAT WE

think about

DREAM BIG

DARE TO

FAIL

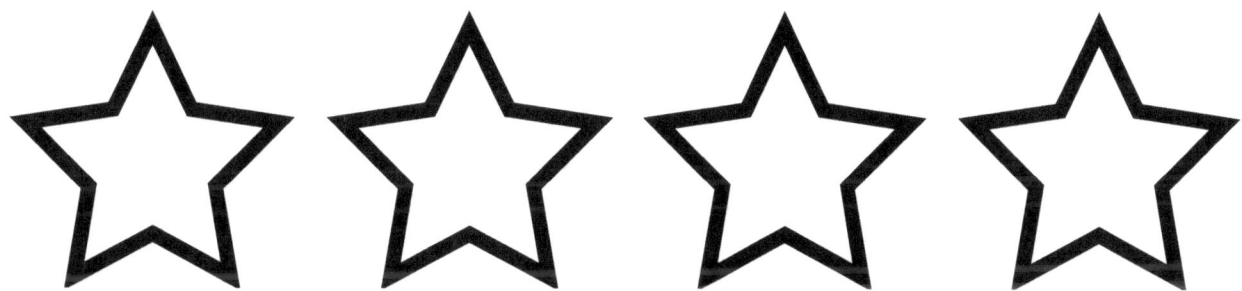

YOU GET
what you
SETTLE FOR

★ ★ ★ ★

LOVE